ITS A HIPPOS WORLD: HIPPOPOTAMUS FUN FACTS FOR KIDS

SPEEDY
PUBLISHING

Speedy Publishing LLC
40 E. Main St. #1156
Newark, DE 19711
www.speedypublishing.com

Hippopotamuses are found in Africa.

The hippopotamus is a large, mostly herbivorous mammal. The name hippopotamus means 'river horse'.

The
hippopotamus
is the third-
largest type of
land mammal.
They grow to
10.8 to 16.5
feet long and
up to 5.2
feet tall.

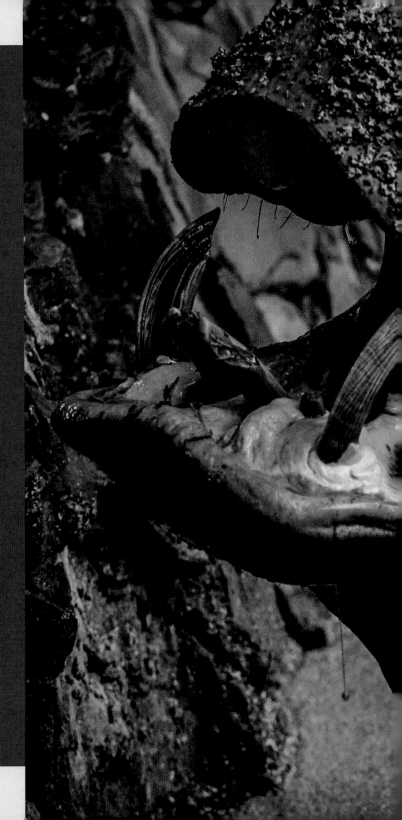

Hippopotamuses spend a large amount of time in water such as rivers, lakes and swamps. Staying submerged helps a hippo stay cool.

Hippopotamuses are social animals, living in groups of up to 30 animals. A group of hippos in known as a 'herd', 'pod', 'dale' or 'bloat'.

A hippo must stay moist, because if its skin dries out, it will crack. Their skin secretes a natural sunscreen substance which is red-coloured.

Hippos can be extremely aggressive, especially if they feel threatened. They are regarded as one of the most dangerous animals in Africa.

A male
hippopotamus
is called a 'bull'
and a female
hippopotamus
is called
a 'cow'.

Made in the USA
Monee, IL
01 May 2020